Published in the UK by
POWERFRESH Limited
21 Rothersthorpe Crescent
Northampton
NN4 8JD

Telephone 0845 130 4565
Facsimile 0845 130 4563
E Mail   info@powerfresh.co.uk

ISBN   1902929268

Printed in Belgium by Proost N.V. International Book Production
Powerfresh September 2002

A Mum's Little
Book of Spells

Spells
for a
Mum-to-be

If you're about to be a new mum
And need some help with what's to come
Then hold this book in your hand
And read aloud these Magical chants...

These Spells come with no guarantees but we wish you lots of luck!

A Spell to Stop
Morning
Sickness

"I'm fed up of feeling sick
And running to the bathroom really quick.
So with the power in this Spell
Make me feel perfectly well.
No more carrots,
No more stew,
No more chucking down the loo."

A Spell to Stop
Cramp

"My husband gets a terrible fright
When in the middle of the night
I get painful cramps that I dread
And nearly kick him clean out of bed.
So I wish for this pain never to come back
So my husband can stop
getting whacked."

A Spell to Get Rid of Back Ache

"I know that every time I awake
This baby will have made me ache
And even though I am so happy
This pain is making me a little snappy.
So I ask this Spell to listen here
And make this pain disappear."

A Spell
to Stop you
Swelling

"My legs and arms feel like balloons
And I look like a character from a cartoon.
So with the power of Fairy Magic
I wish for my life to not be so tragic.
I want to become perfectly thin
Without ugly, bloated, stretched skin."

A Spell to Get Rid of Hot Weather

"I normally love it to be nice and warm
But this Summer I'm wishing for
a snow storm.
So I wish for a blizzard to keep me cool
Or my own personal swimming pool."

A Spell to Help you Sleep

"How am I supposed to sleep in my bed
Now my tummy is risen like a huge
loaf of bread.
It's like sleeping with a cannon ball
But one that kicks your stomach wall.
So I wish to sleep on a bed of
feathers and air
And stop my constant nightmare."

A Spell for a Quick and Easy Labour

"The last nine months now seem easy
But the thought of the birth makes me
feel queasy.
So I wish for it all to go really quick
And not be a long painful epic.
So with the help of this Magic Rhyme
Give me a healthy baby
In double quick time."

Spells for a New Mum

If you have just become a new mummy
And need some help now it's
out of your tummy
Then hold this book in your hand
And read aloud these Magical chants...

These Spells come with no guarantees but we wish you lots of luck!

A Spell to Magically Change Nappies

"It's not easy being a new mother
As my life is one dirty nappy after another.
So save me changing any more bums
With this Magic Spell's outcome.
No more nappies to replace,
And no more peeing in my face."

A Spell to Get Rid of Baby Sick

"Alakazam, Alakazear,
Make this stain disappear
And with the help of
this Magic Spell
Remove this horrible, putrid smell."

A Spell for a Good Night's Sleep

"I call upon the Magic Sandman
To stir a potion in his cauldron
To help us with our sleepless plight
And make our baby sleep
through the night.
So no more screaming at 1 o'clock
And no more bottles at 2,3,4,4.30
and 5 o'clock."

An Understanding Crying Spell

"I know babies have to cry
But I'd love to magically know why.
Is it a dirty nappy or empty tummy
Or just the need for a soothing dummy.
So I ask for the help of a kindly fairy
To make it all a lot less scary.
So next time I hear a yell
I'll know if they are ill or well."

A Spell to Magically Make Baby Bottles

"Eight bottles a day to sterilise and fill
Is starting to lose it's initial thrill.
So I call upon Ancient Magic
To make this task not as tragic.
Keep my fridge well stacked up
With fresh bottled milk for my baby to sup."

A Spell for a Night Out

"Since our beautiful baby was born
I've stayed in from dusk till dawn.
So I command the power of a
partying Sprite
To give me a fantastic, groovy night.
With no more worries and no more stress
As we leave our child with which we are
blessed."

A Spell
to Stop Smelly,
Pooey Nappies

"It looks like nuclear waste
A glowing, green, runny paste
And I need this really strong Spell
To protect me from the acrid smell.
So I'd like to feel much more happy
Next time I open a pooey nappy.
Make it a pretty colour
Make it smell sweet
Not like the groin of a sweaty athlete."

A Spell to
Empty the
Wash Basket

"My washing machine is feeling the strain
With the piles of clothes my baby stains.
So I think it's time to give it a rest
From washing hundreds of baby grows
and vests.
So make all his clothes stay
magically clean
With no sick or poo stains to be seen."

A Spell to Get Rid of Ironing

"My ironing pile is now two storeys high
And makes me want to break down and cry.
So make it all magically disappear
With no more steam, sweat or tears.
Then keep the pile permanently low
So I don't wear out my elbow."

A Spell to Stop Toddlers Banging their Heads

"I watch my toddler with fear and dread
As I know he'll yet again bang his head.
He never looks where he is going
And the dints in the furniture are now showing.
So I wish for some Magic to protect
His precious, beautiful, little head.
No more bumps, no more lumps
Each time he goes with a thump."

A Spell to Stop Toddlers Climbing

"My toddler climbs everything
Like a miniature Sherpa Tensing.
So with this potion from a Magic Fairy
Stop him behaving so scary.
Keep his feet firmly on the ground
No longer heading upward bound."

A Spell to Understand Gibberish

"My baby is beginning to say some words
But it is like nothing before I've ever heard.
So I need this translation Spell
to make clear
All this gibberish that I hear.
No more 'eh oh'
And no more 'de da dum'
Just a sweet ' I love you Mum'."

A Spell to Help with the Terrible Twos

"Now my baby has reached the
terrible twos
I've realised all the rumours were true.
She is completely out of control
Like some monstrous little Troll.
So with the help of this Calming Spell
Make our home a nicer place to dwell.
No more tantrums, no more screams
Just a child who's a complete dream."

An Anti-Tantrum Spell

"My toddler keeps having a public tantrum
Screaming for sweets as he falls
on his bum.
So I wish to become much stronger
And not put up with this any longer.
Then the next time he heads for the floor
One look and he'll know I'm
laying down the law."

Spells for a Mum with Young Children

If as a mum you need a break
From all the trouble your kids make
Then hold this book in your hand
And read aloud these Magical chants...

These Spells come with no guarantees but we wish you lots of luck!

An Anti-Farting Spell

"My kid thinks farting is really fun
And falls about laughing when he drops one
But I wish he'd be a bit more shrewd
About who he insults when being so rude.
So I wish for a Magic Cork for his bum
Then he can no longer part with
a smelly one."

A Spell to Stop Kids Eating with their Mouth Open

"My kid can't eat with his mouth shut
And we have to watch what's heading
for his gut.
So I wish for this Spell to close his lips
Next time he has fish fingers and chips.
Then I'll no longer need to blush
As everyone watches him chew
unsightly mush."

An
Anti-Dropsies
Spell

"My kid drops everything everywhere
Without a thought or even a care
And I've just about had enough
Of picking up clothes and
personal stuff.
So I wish for a really powerful Spell
To make things rise from where they fell.
Make my home clean, make my home neat
Not like some littered, old, scruffy street."

A Spell for Good Manners

"How much does a 'Please' and
'Thank You' cost
As my kid's manners seem to be lost.
So with the help of this Magic Spell
I'd like them to learn manners really well.
No more 'umphs', no more 'ehs'
Just 'Yes Thank You'
and 'Please' instead."

A Spell to Get Kids to Brush their Teeth

"My child won't use a toothbrush
To clean his teeth inside his mush.
So I ask the wise old Tooth Fairy
To make him realise just how scary
Chewing with only gums really is
When you've been fitted with falsies."

A Washing Spell

"My kid is scared of water and soap
And I am starting to give up all hope.
So with the help of a fairy's grace
I wish for my child to wash his face.
Then no more grime behind his ears
And no more necks covered in
mud smears."

A Spell
to Stop
Nose Picking

"No adult understands or knows
A kid's obsession with their nose
They are always picking at their
bogies and snot
Tunnelling away to see what they've got.
So I wish for my kid to give it more thought
And not entertain me with this sport."

A Washing Up Spell

"As we don't have a dish washing machine
It's time to get the kids to clean.
But it starts to become a real drag
When I'm always being told I'm a nag.
So with a magic daisy and yellow buttercup
I wish to make the kids desperate
to wash up."

A Cuddling Spell

"My child now thinks she is too old
To let me pick her up and hold.
So Piddle, Paddle, Puddle
Make my child still want a cuddle.
Let me be able to give her a squeeze
Without her thinking she'll
catch a disease."

A Spell to Keep a Bed Made

"I feel like my kids' personal slave
Because their beds are never made.
So Alakazam, Alakazear
Make this mess disappear.
Fluff the pillows,
Tuck in the sheets
And hide the marks from their mucky feet."

EVERYTHING
YOU NEED
TO KNOW
IN JUST
10 MINS

A Spell to Make Homework Easy

"My kids are sick of all their homework
And they are starting to drive me berserk.
So Ipsy, Dypsy, Lemon Squeezy.
Make their homework quick and easy.
Keep it all short and sweet
Then they don't feel the need to cheat.
And with the power in this rhyme
Help them have more free time."

Spells
for a
Mum of
Teenagers

If your life has become very strange
Now your kids have hit the teenage change
Then hold this book in your hand
And read aloud these Magical chants...

These Spells come with no guarantees but we wish you lots of luck!

A Spell to Help you Understand Teenagers

"My kids have become a real nightmare
And every conversation includes a glare.
They are always whining or grunting at me
And never want to eat their tea.
I need to understand their every mood
And so be calm when they are rude.
So with this Understanding Spell
Help make my life less like hell."

A Spell to Get your Kids to Listen to you

"My kids have developed a problem
with their ears
As I don't seem able to make myself clear.
They've become very good at ignoring me
So I ask this Spell to hear my plea.
Next time I say 'Tidy this'
It's done so quick I'm left speechless."

A Spell to Enjoy your Kid's Music

"In my head I hear thud, thud, thud.
No words, no rhythm, but who would.
So I ask this Spell to help me out
And leave me with absolutely no doubt
That the music I hear pounding
through her wall
Is more than a screeching caterwaul."

An
Anti-Fuddy Duddy
Spell

"With the help of this powerful Spell
I'd like me and my kids to really gel.
No more thinking I'm too old to understand
The lyrics and music of their favourite band
Or that I think it's no big deal
The way that life makes them feel."

A Spell
to Get Rid of
B.O.

"My kid has developed smelly armpits
But hasn't yet realised it.
The smell of onions is really strong
And I wish she'd notice the
atrocious pong.
So with this Magical Fairy Spell
Help me with this unpleasant smell.
Make her use the deodorant I bought
So she no longer smells like a fishing port."

A Spell to Get Rid of Greasy Hair

"My teenager's hair is really lanky
And the grease makes it look very manky.
But she doesn't seem to be aware
That she needs to regularly wash her hair.
So with this Magic held here unseen
Keep her hair permanently clean.
No longer the need for a paper bag
on her head.
Just shining, glossy hair instead."

A Spell to Keep a Kid's Room Tidy

"My kid's floor is a rubbish tip
And the room looks like the
inside of a skip.
So Alakazam, Alakazear
Make this mess disappear.
Straighten the bed,
Clear the floor
And put the clothes back in the drawer."

A Spell to Stop Spot Squeezing

"My kid is obsessed with squeezing spots
Probably because she's got such a lot.
But I'm tired of the mirrors being a mess
With signs of all her squeezing success.
So I wish for her to have perfectly
clear skin
With no more squeezable zit fountains."

A Spell for a Moody Teenager

"My child now only knows three words
And our conversations have become absurd.
All we hear is 'Taxi', 'Money' and 'Food'
As she sulks around in a teenage mood.
So towards her this Spell direct
And make her treat us with more respect.
So no more demands on our love
and good will
And no more looks that could easily kill."

A Spell for Boyfriend Vetting

"My daughter is now dating boys
And it's not something we enjoy.
So with the help of this Magic Spell
Help us sort the angels from the
spawn of hell.
We only want the best for her
And boyfriends who we prefer."

A Spell to Clear the Bathroom

"Now my child has hit a certain age
She's hit the bathroom hogging stage
And the rest of the family are
starting to stink
Because we can't get near the
bath or sink.
So I ask the Fairy of all that's clean
To make her rush her preening routine."

A Spell for a Text Maniac

"My daughter is always texting her mates
To arrange school and important dates.
But the bills are now enormously high
And make her dad want to cry.
So I ask the powers of everything technical
To make her phone incredibly Magical.
So when she wants she can text for free
And not make paupers of her dad and me."